I0465111

Adult Coloring book Chickens

Vol 1

By: L. M. Boelz

I want to take a moment to thank you for purchasing this coloring book.

A lot of time went into the making of it. I wanted to be able to give you hours of fun

and relaxation, so enjoy. Be sure to check out my other coloring books if you

like this one. There are 15 different pictures to color in this book.

Other titles

Southwest, Mandalas, Floral

pages

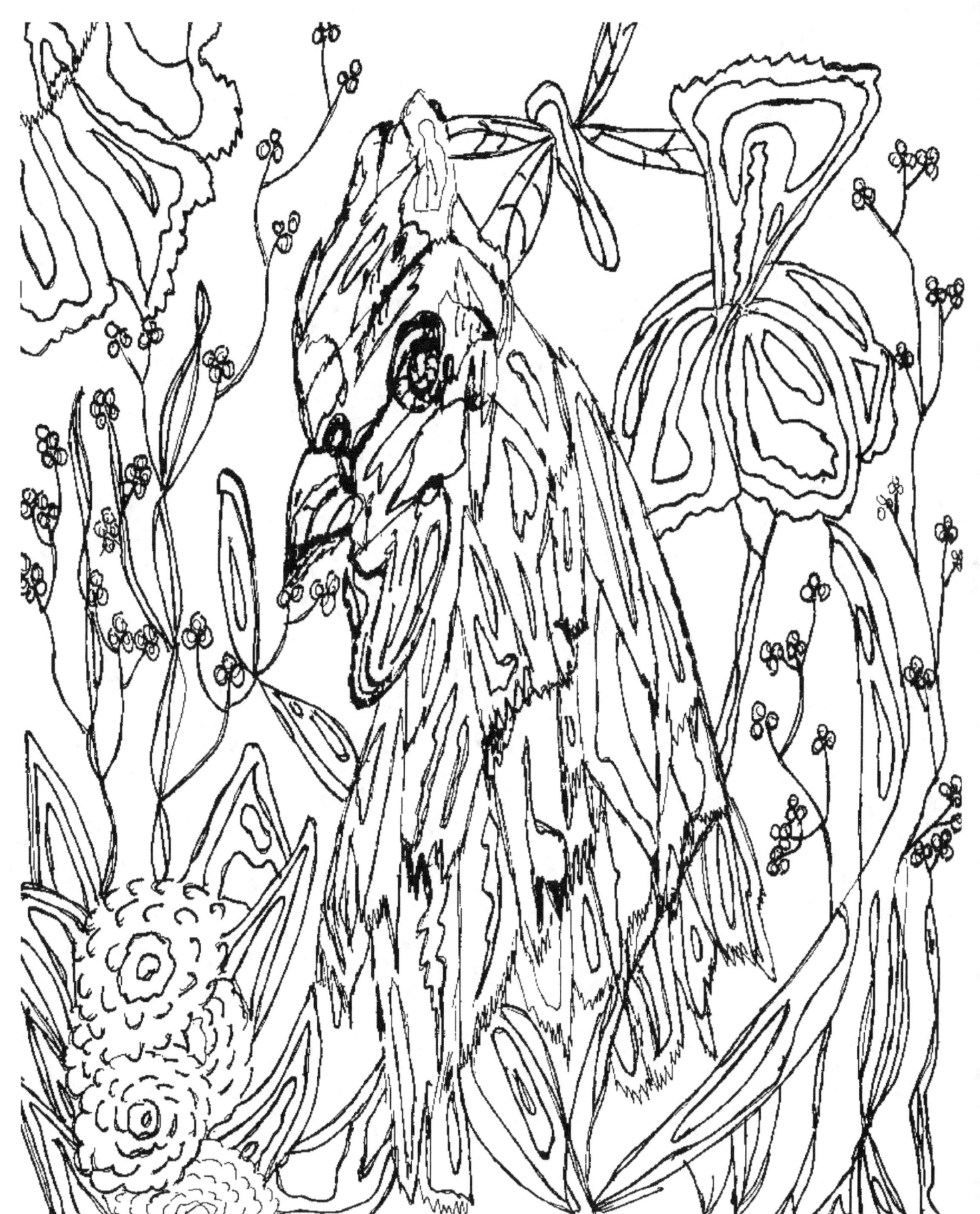

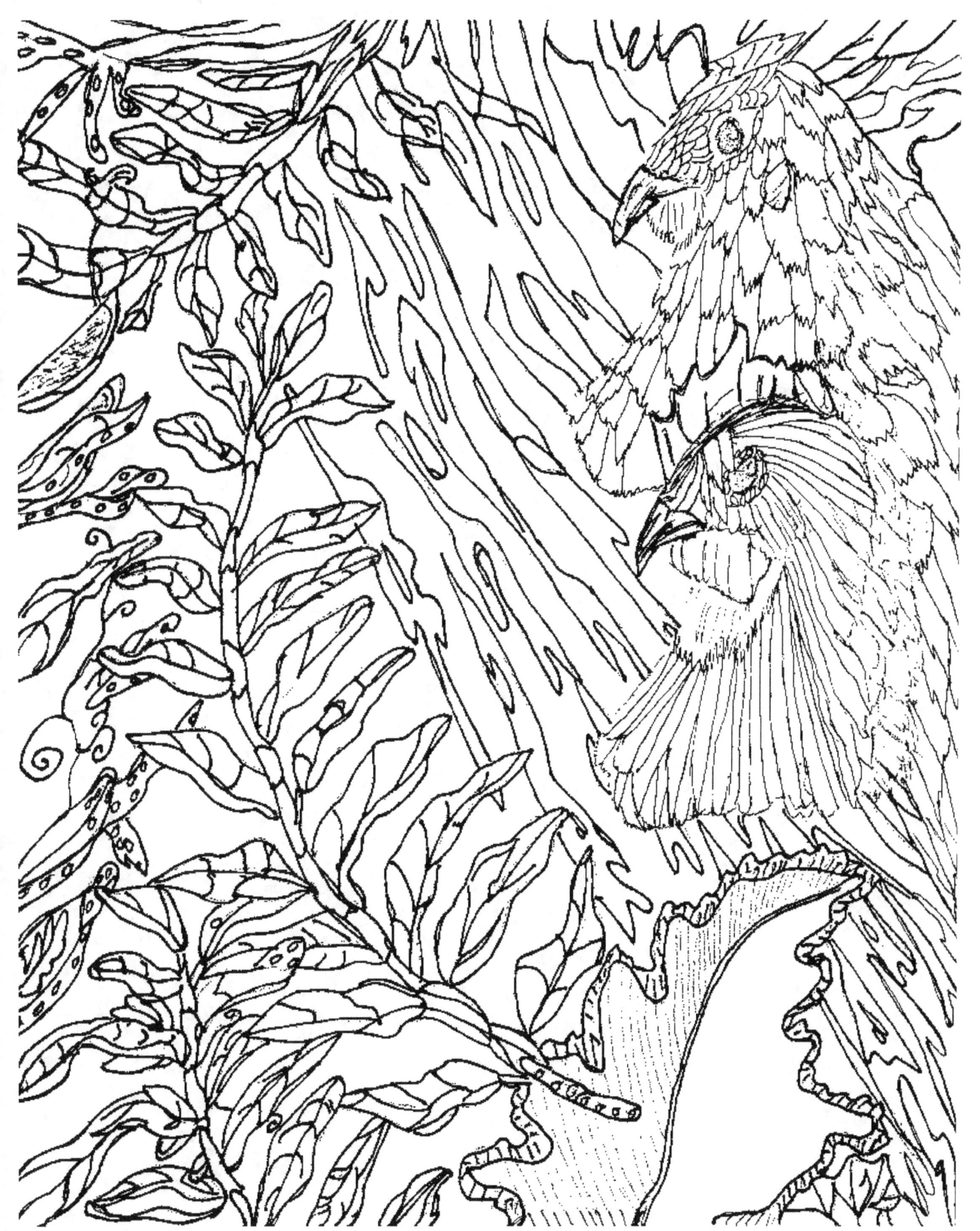

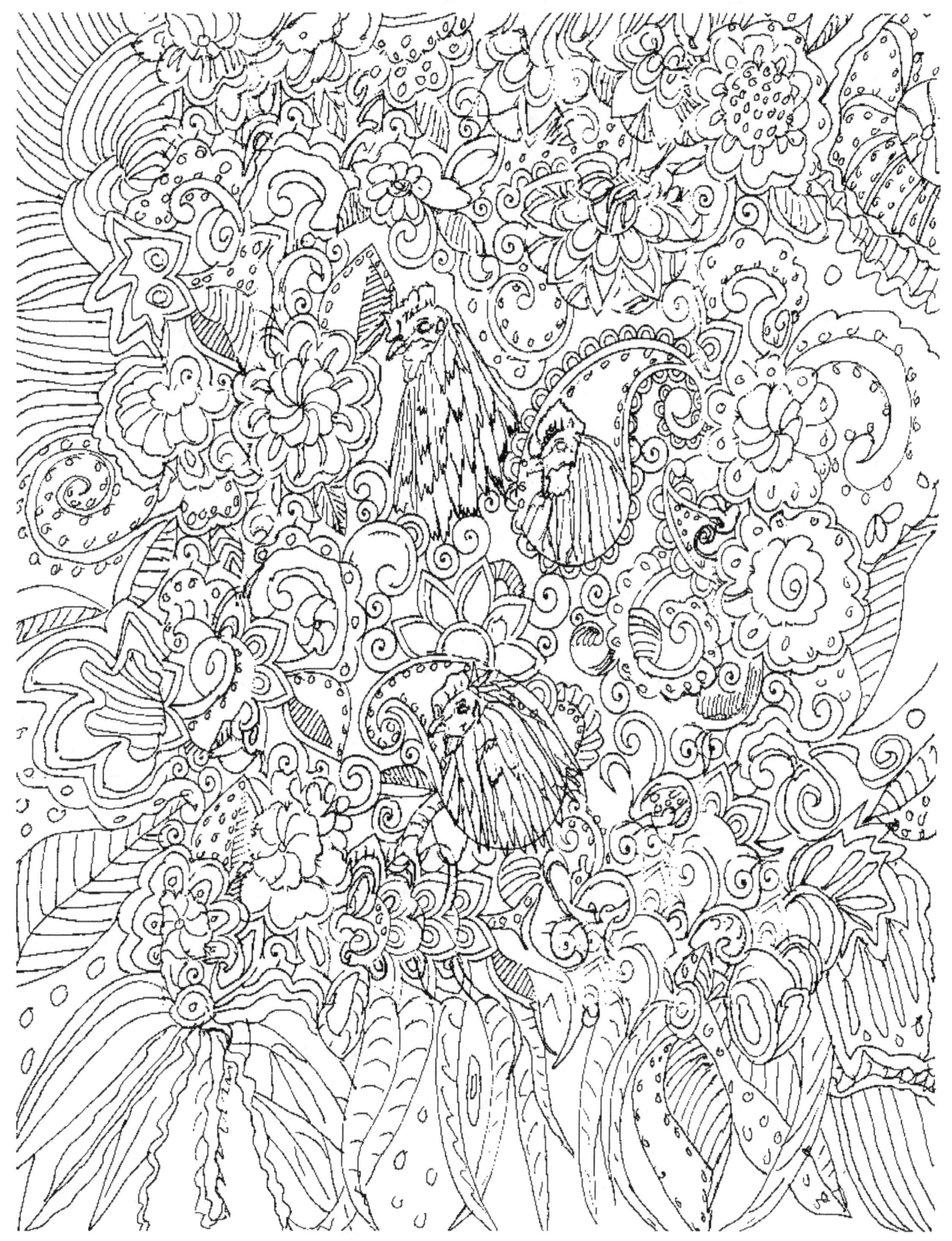

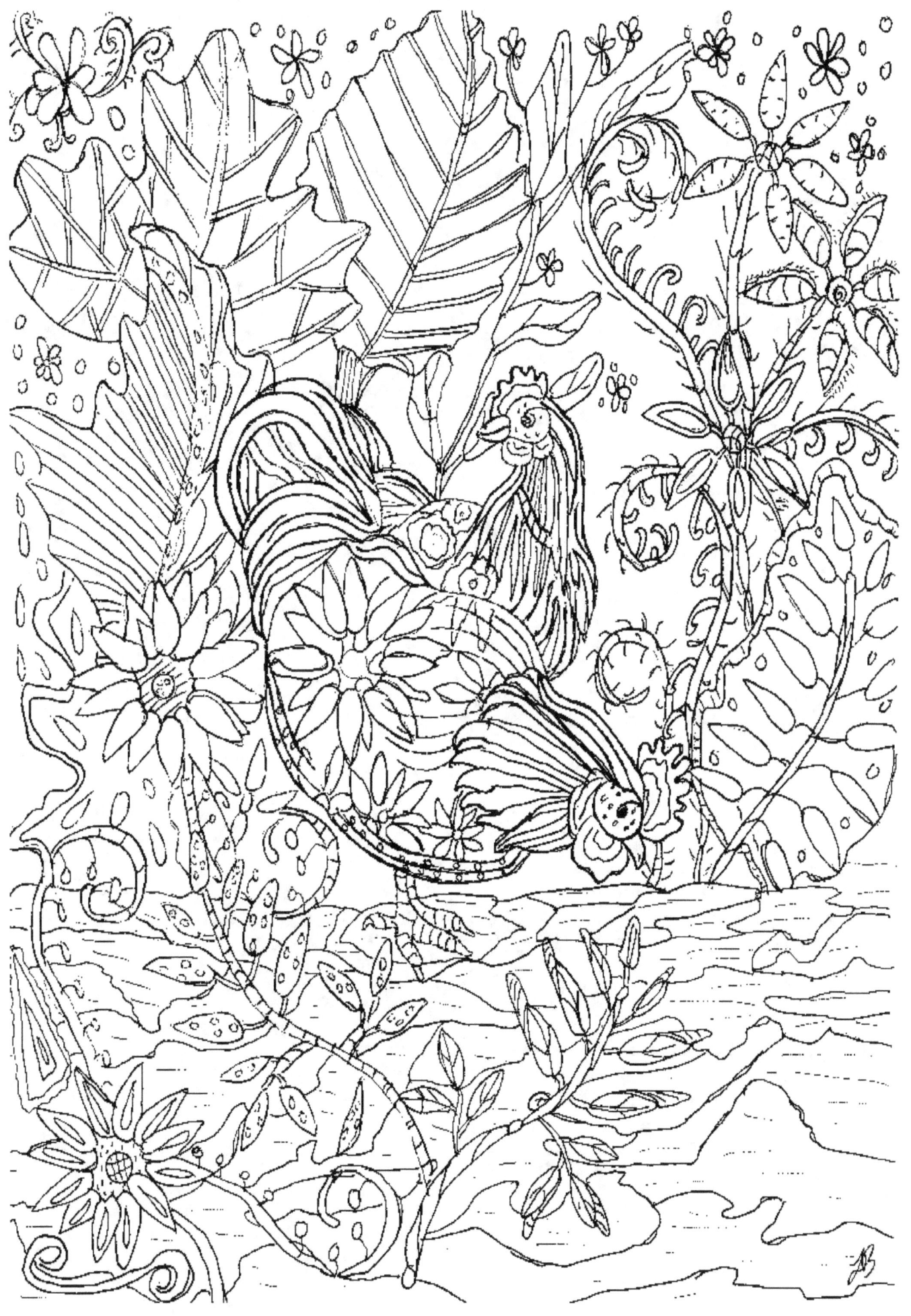

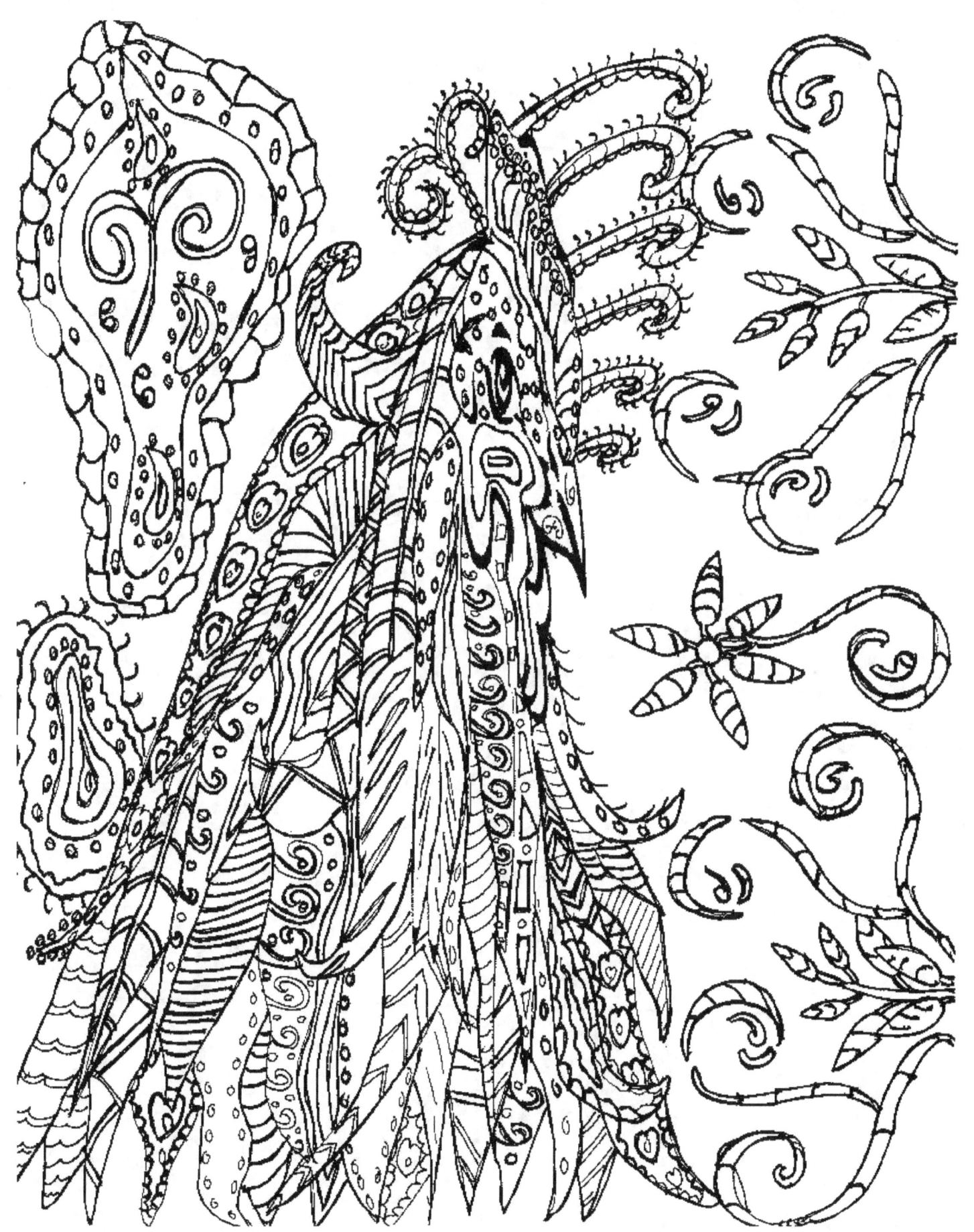

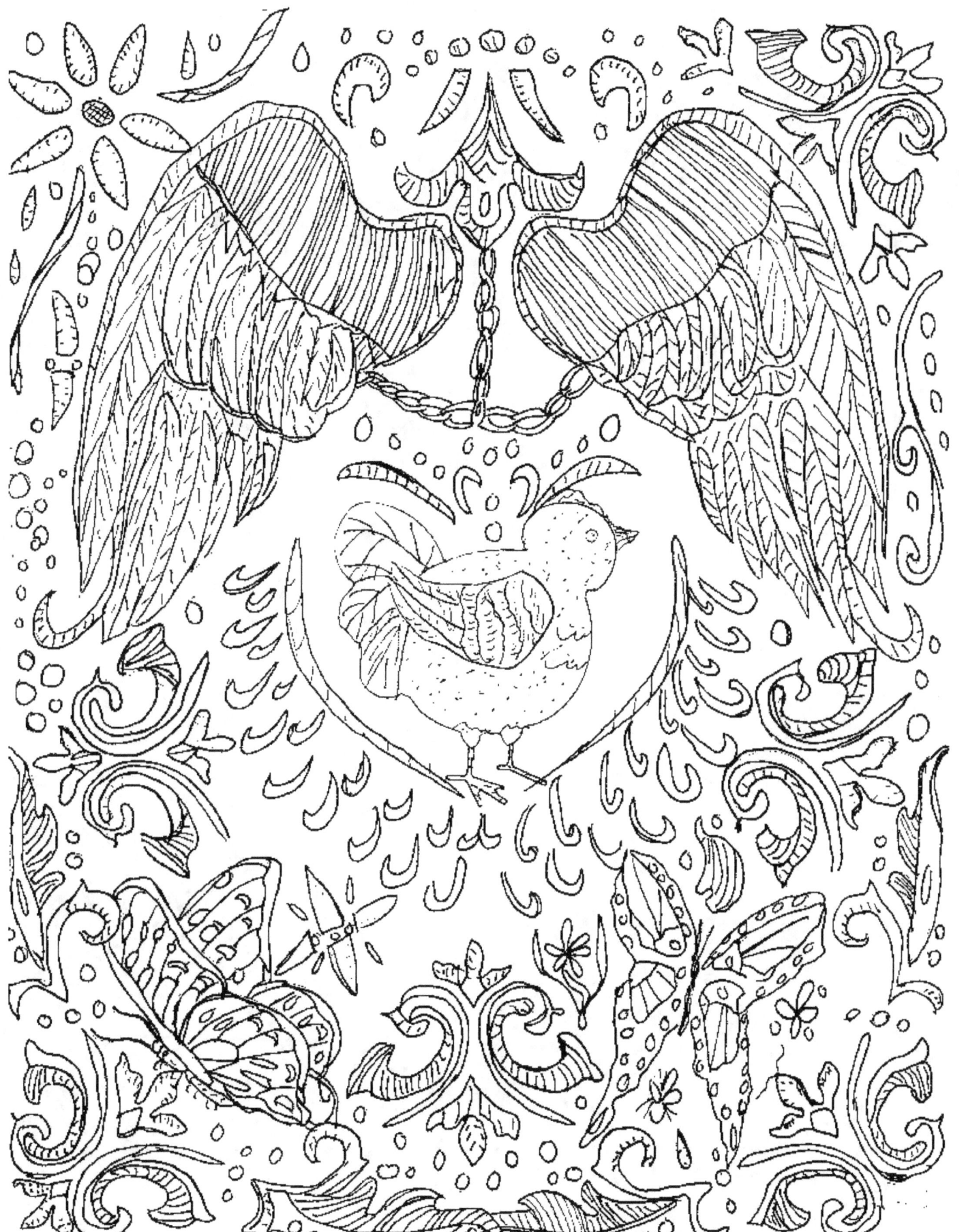

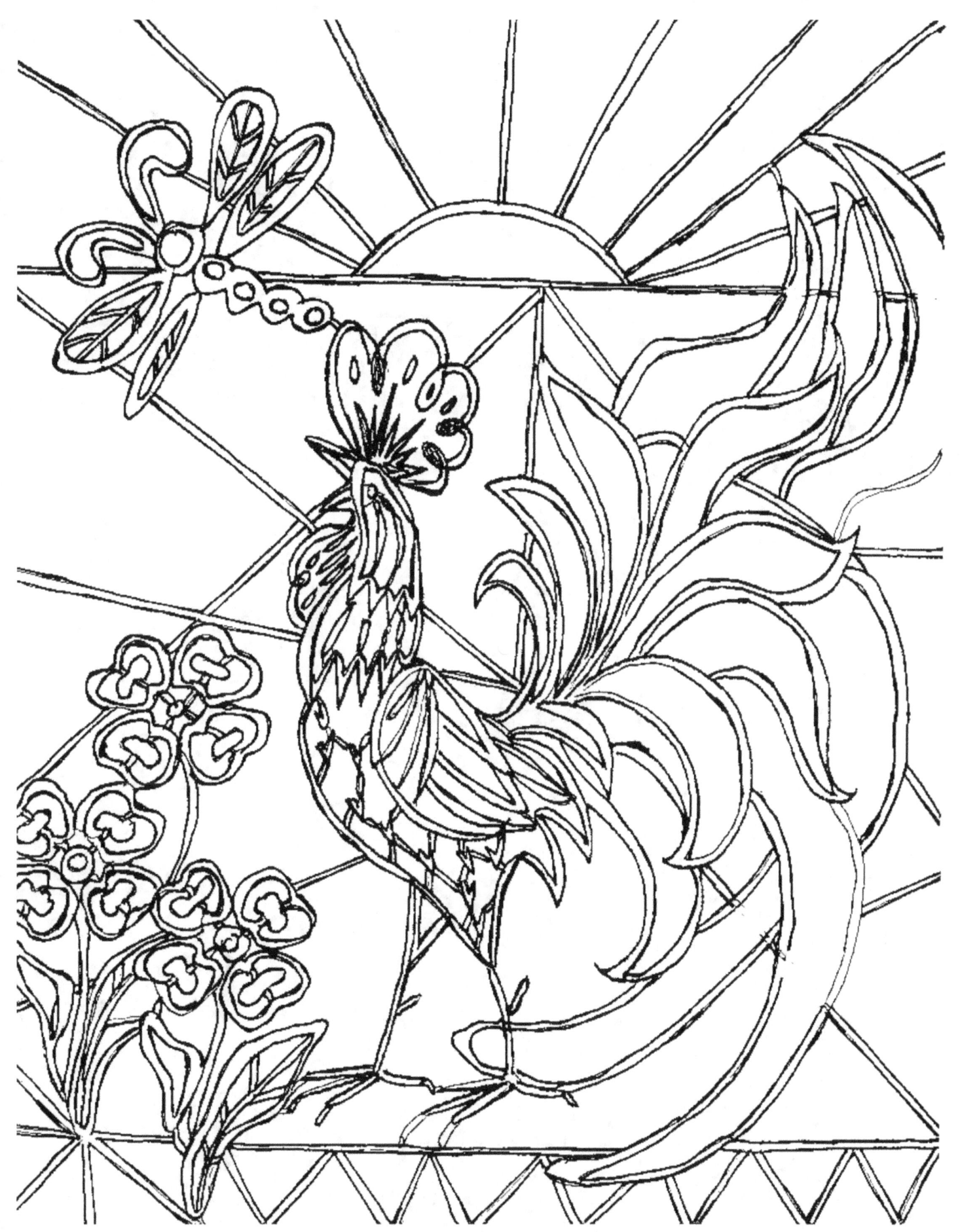

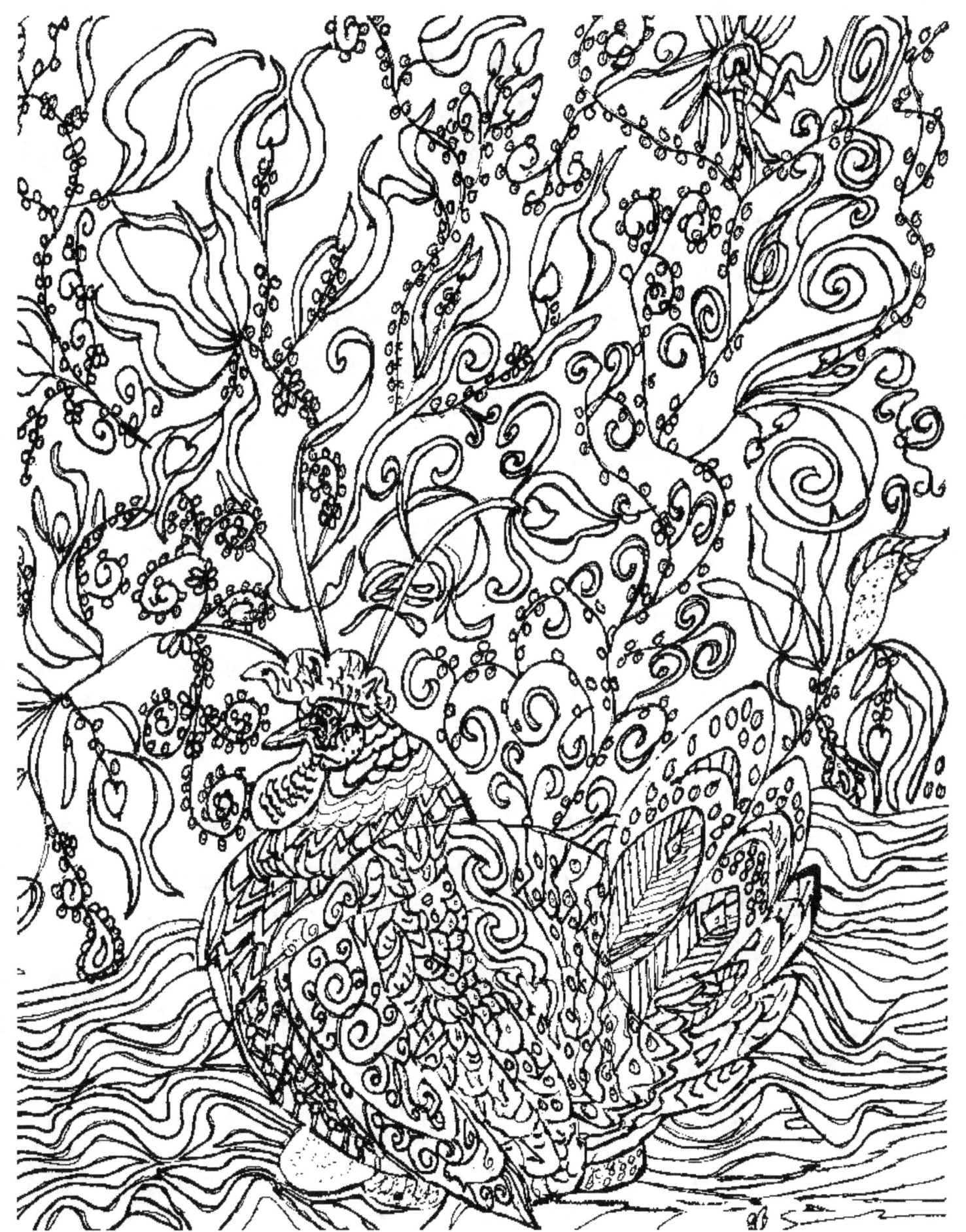

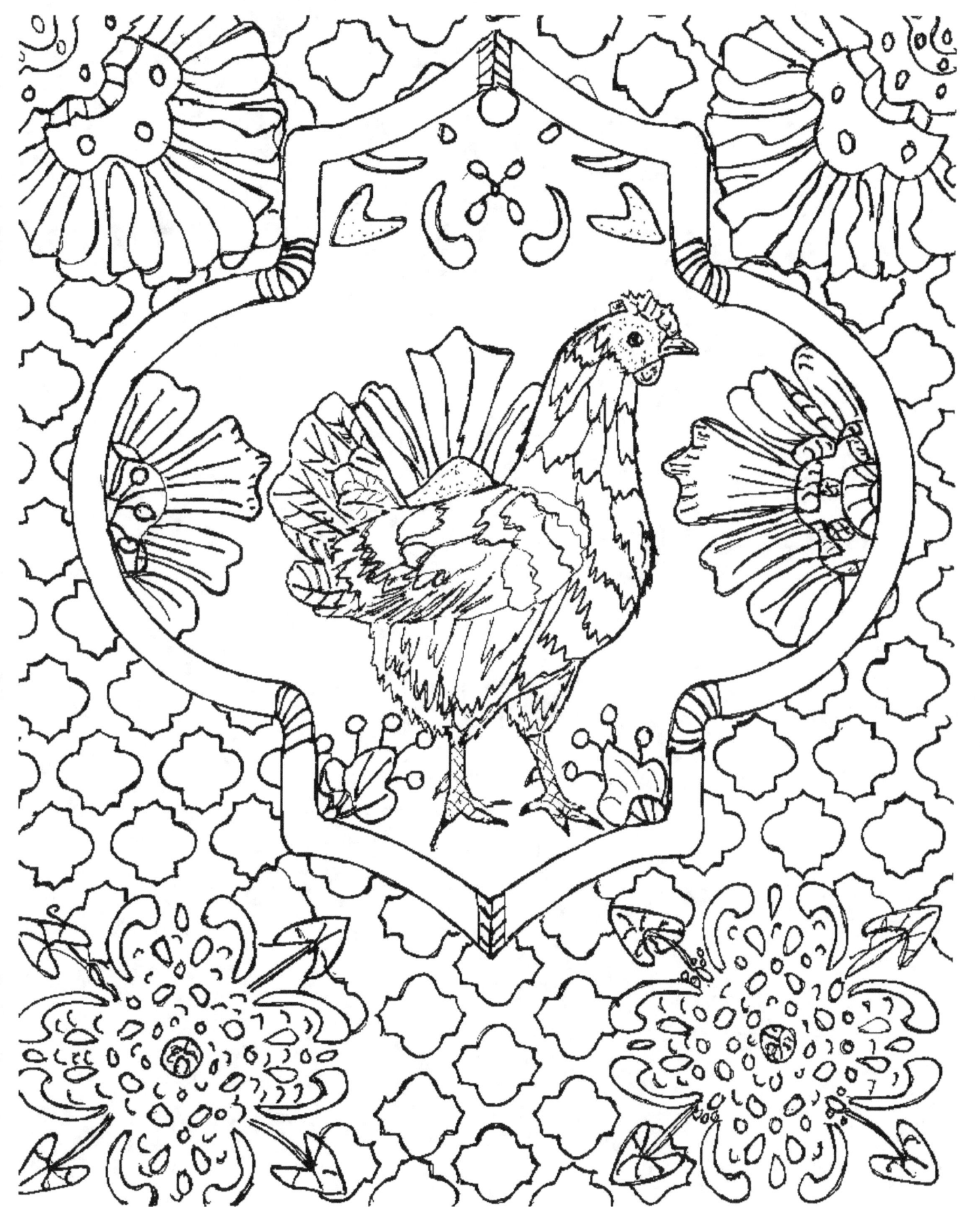

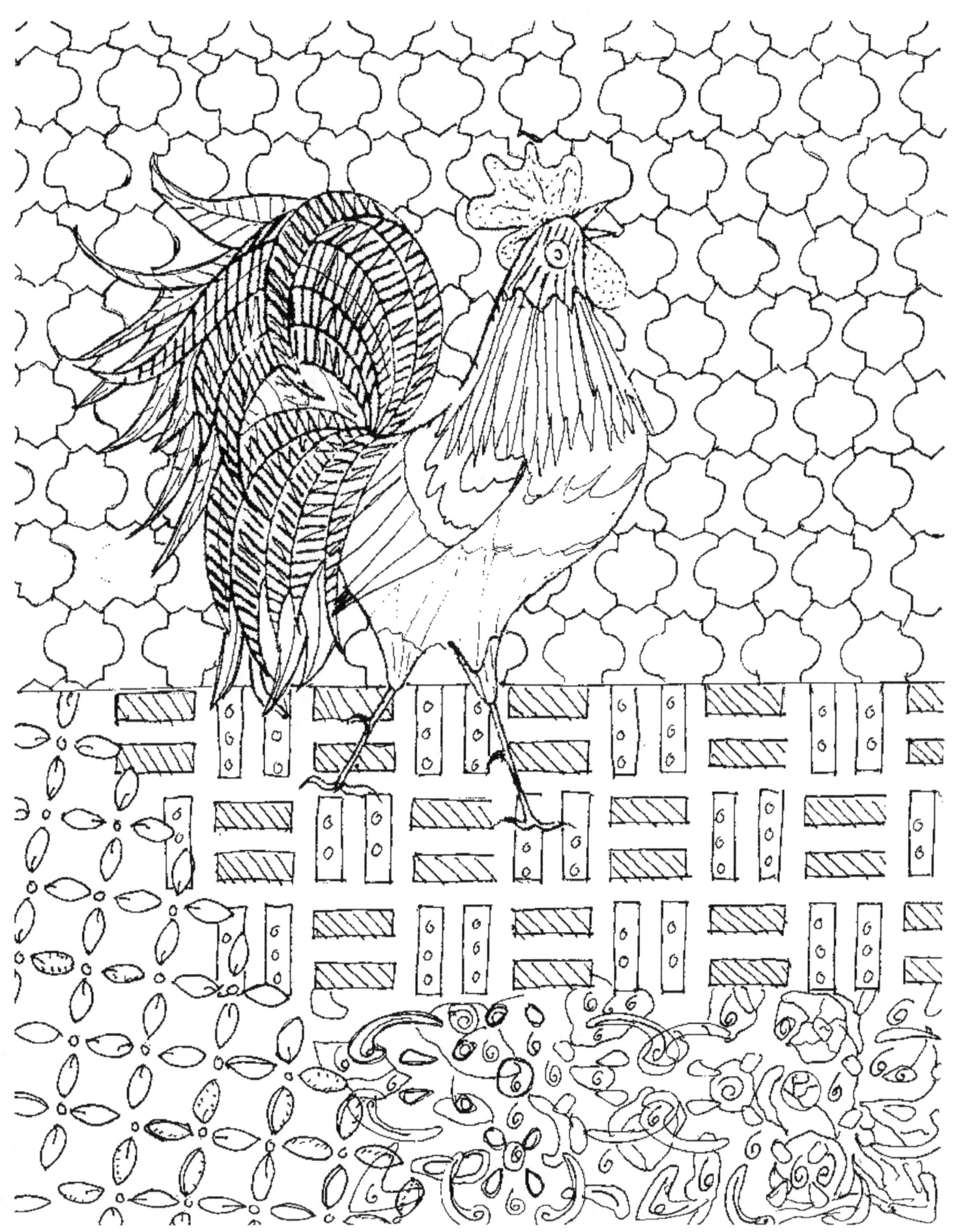

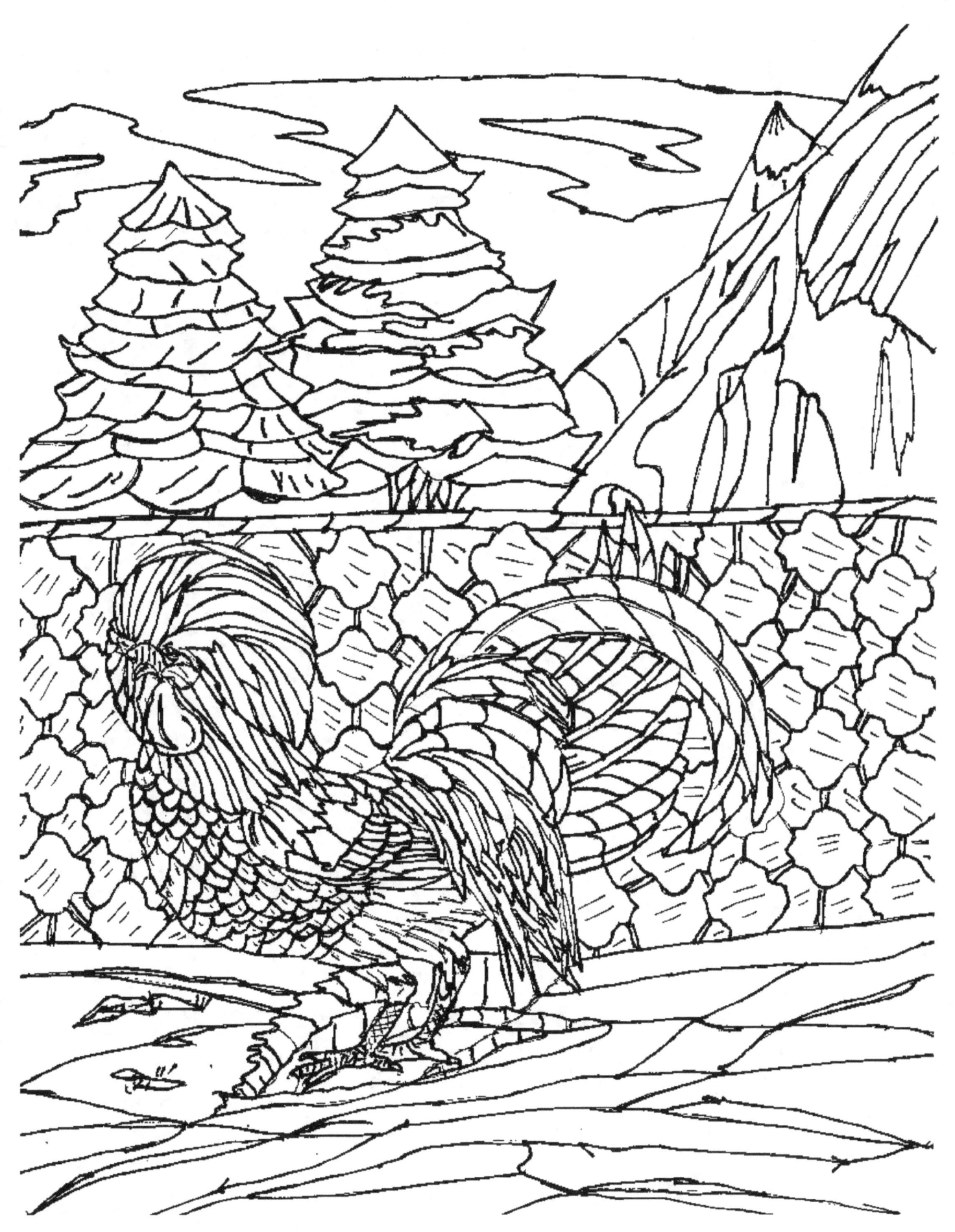

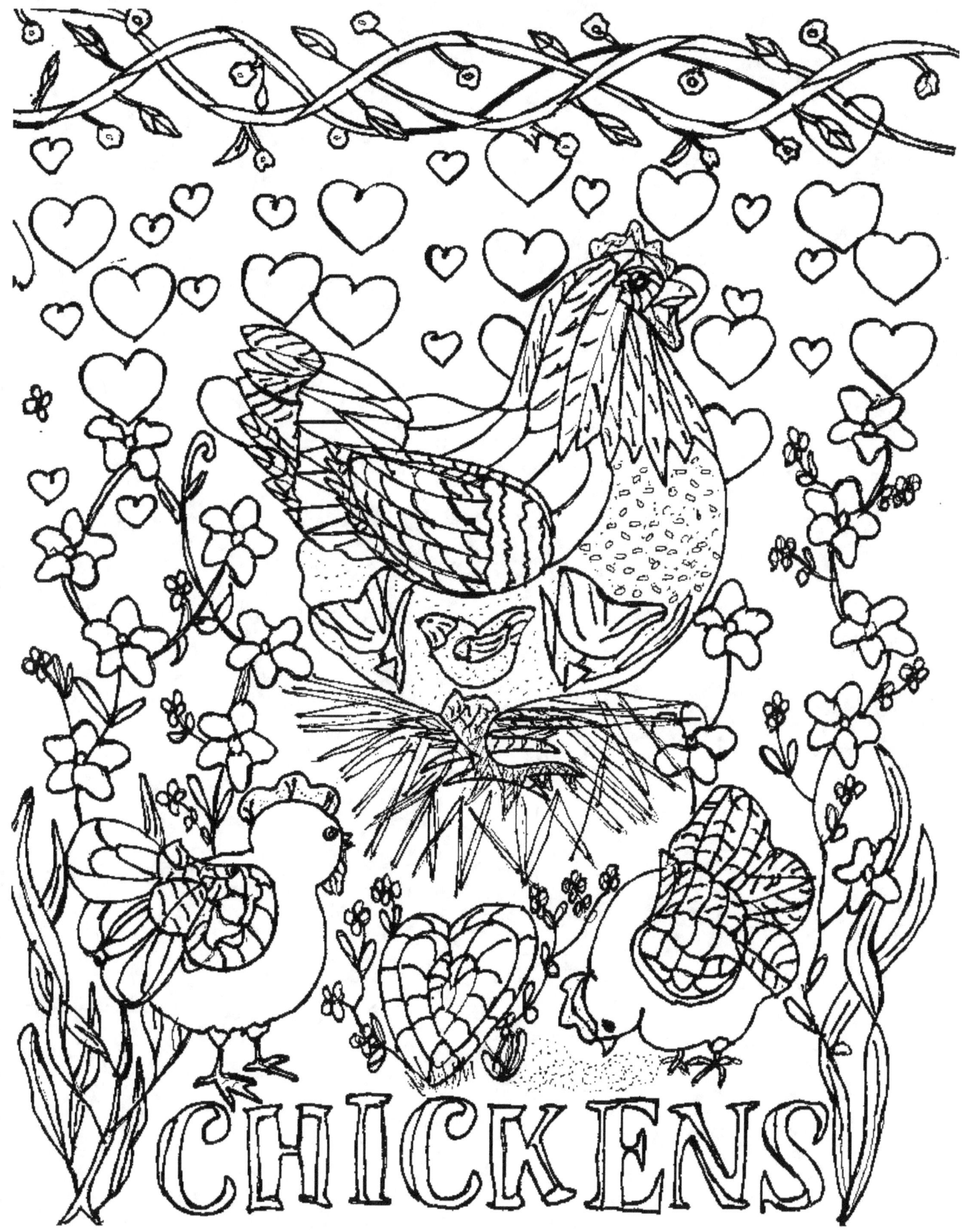

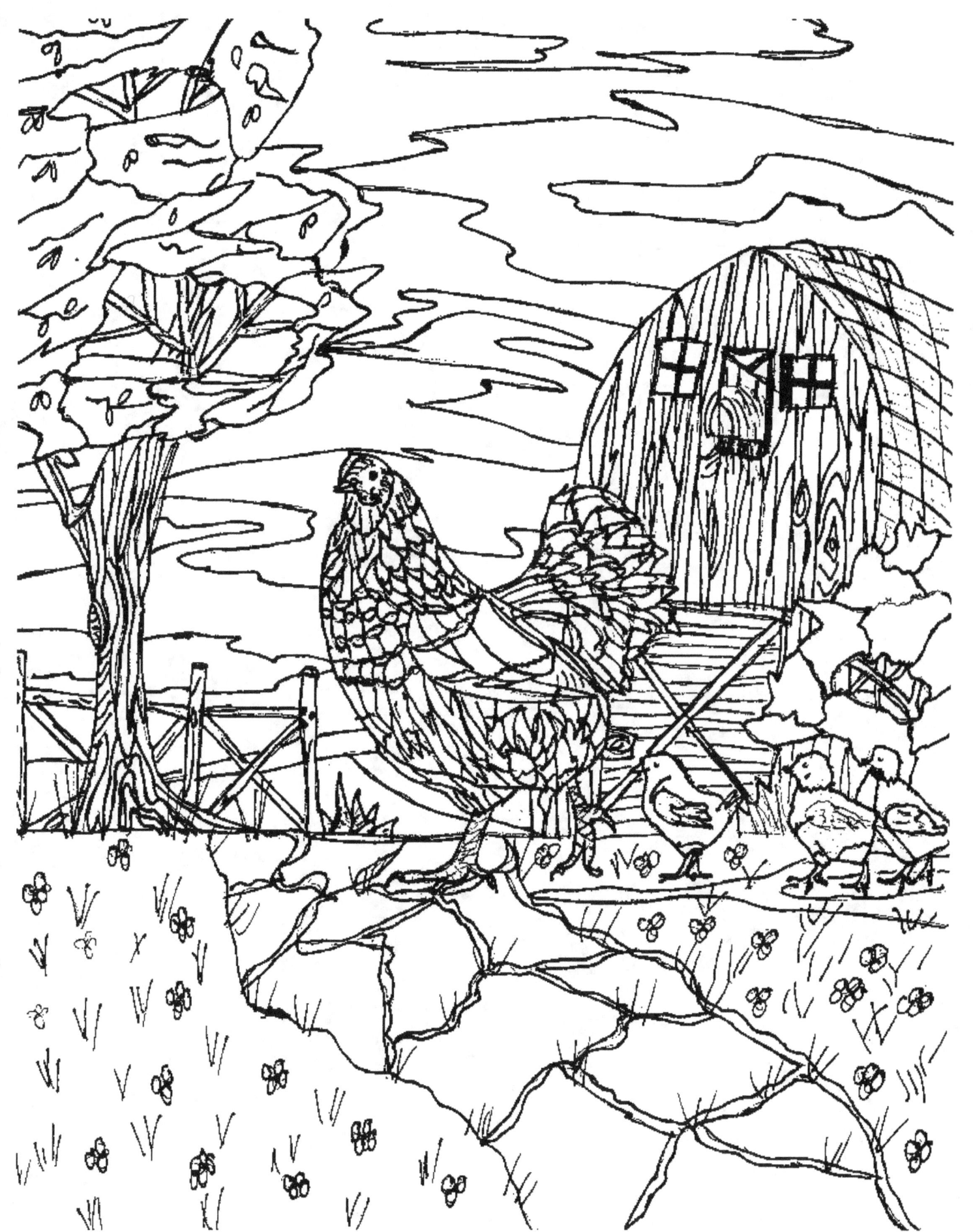

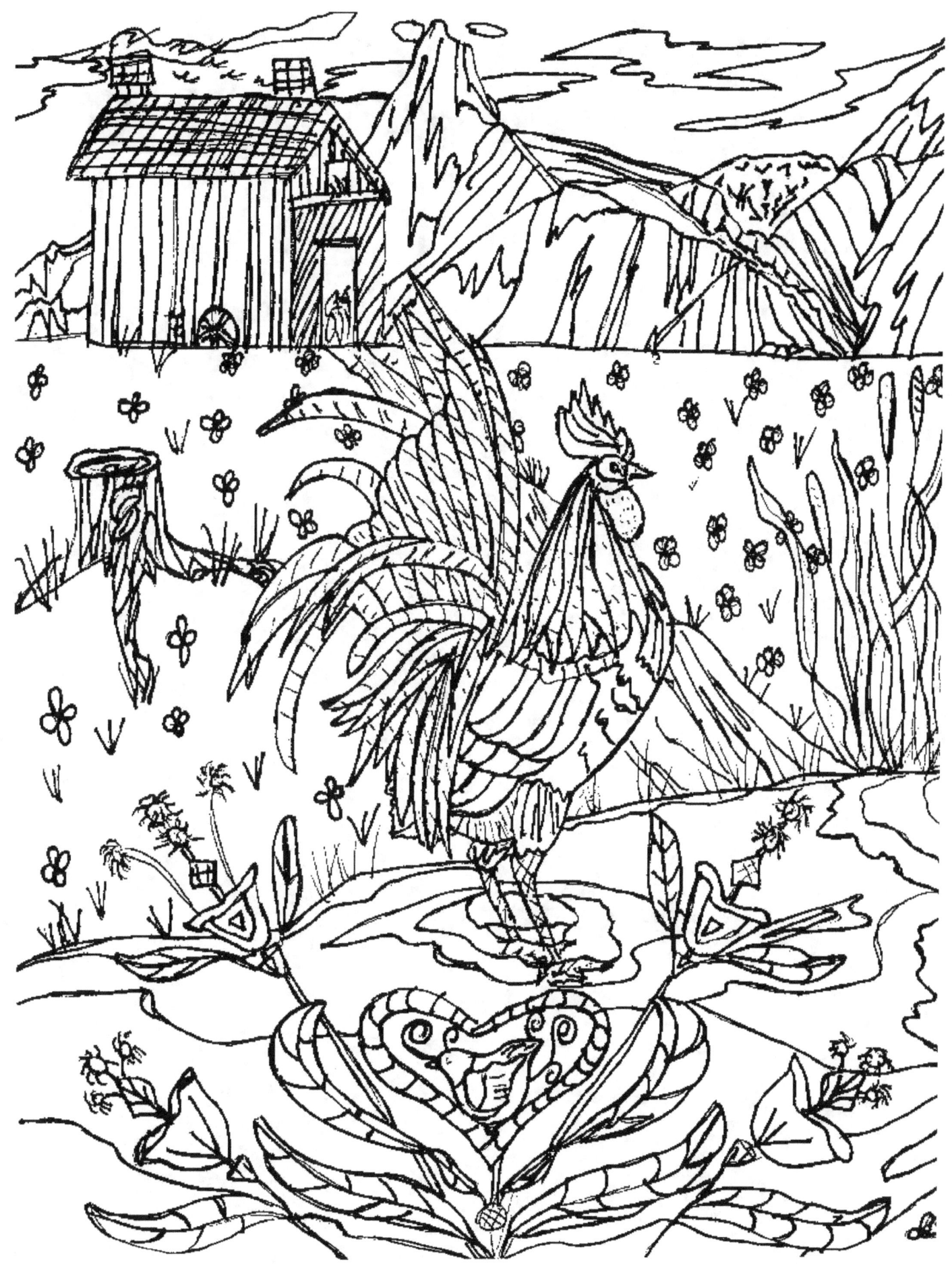

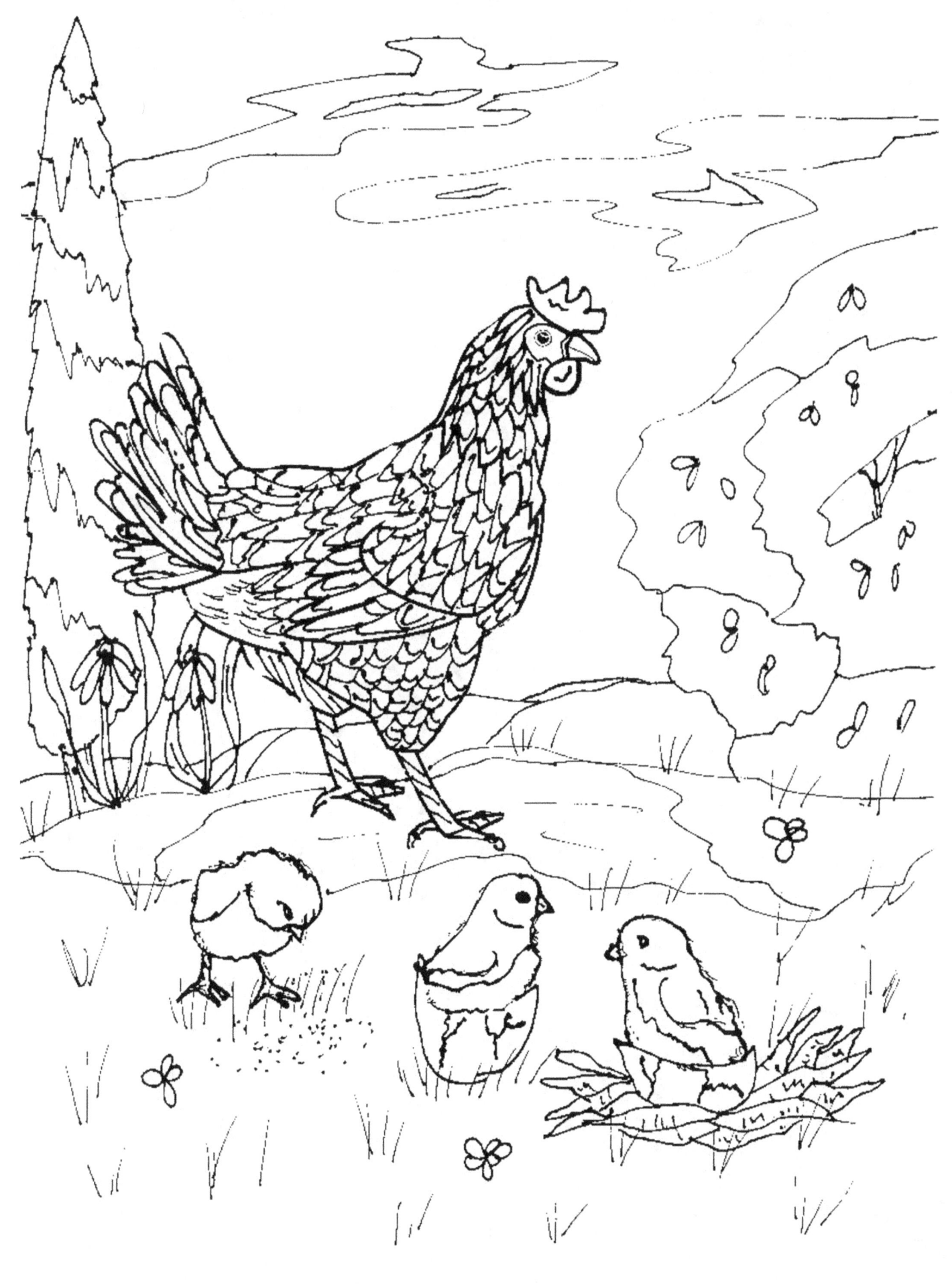